So You're on the Search Committee

Other Titles on Pastoral Transitions from the Alban Institute

A Change of Pastors...and How It Affects Change in the Congregation
by Loren B. Mead

New Beginnings: The Pastorate Start-up Book
by Roy Oswald

Beginning Ministry Together: The Alban Handbook for Clergy Transitions
by Roy M. Oswald, James M. Heath, and Ann W. Heath

Revitalizing Congregations: Refocusing and Healing through Pastoral Transitions
by William O. Avery

Saying Goodbye: A Time of Growth for Congregations and Pastors
by Edward A. White

The Alban Guide to Managing the Pastoral Search Process
by John Vonhof

Temporary Shepherds: A Congregational Handbook for Interim Ministry
edited by S. Roger Nicholson

So You're on the Search Committee

Bunty Ketcham
with Celia Allison Hahn

An Alban Institute Book
ROWMAN & LITTLEFIELD
Lanham • Boulder • New York • Toronto • Plymouth, UK

Copyright © 2005 by the Alban Institute.

First Rowman & Littlefield paperback edition 2014

Published by Rowman & Littlefield
4501 Forbes Blvd, Suite 200, Lanham, MD 20706
www.rowman.com

10 Thornbury Road
Plymouth PL6 7PP
United Kingdom

Library of Congress Cataloging-in-Publication Data Available

ISBN 13: 978-1-56699-316-6 (pbk: alk. paper)

☻™ The paper used in this publication meets the minimum requirements of American National Standard for Information Sciences—Permanence of Paper for Printed Library Materials, ANSI/NISO Z39.48-1992.

Printed in the United States of America

Cover design by Adele Robey, Phoenix Graphics.

Author's Note

So You're on the Search Committee began its life as a conversation between Celia Allison Hahn, then the editor-in-chief at the Alban Institute, and myself regarding this crucial transition stage in the lives of congregations and laypersons' special role therein. The edited conversation was first published in booklet form by Alban in 1985 and went through multiple printings over its eighteen-year life. This version, while retaining the original book's interview format, includes significant updates and revisions based on my subsequent experience in consulting with congregations going through pastoral transitions.

This conversation takes place within the context of one institution—the church. My hope is that all persons responsible for the renewal of their organization through change of leadership will eavesdrop with interest.

Bunty Ketcham
March 2005

So You're on the Search Committee

Bunty, as you know, the Alban Institute has developed a lot of help for the search process over the years. Many of the resources were written for ordained professionals of one kind or another, such as judicatory executives, consultants, and interim pastors who help the search committee do its job. But it's the laity who really carry out the search process in all except Catholic and United Methodist churches. You are not only a layperson who is a trained and experienced consultant, but you have also served on multiple search committees. Out of that fortuitous mix, what are some of the most important pieces of advice that you would want to offer members of the committee?

I think I'd like first to send, not advice, but a message to **REWARDS** people who have said, "Yes, I'll be on the search committee." Taking on this responsibility is an act of faith on your part and one for which you will be rewarded. I have recently asked some people who have gone through this long, demanding, sometimes tedious process just what it was that sustained and rewarded them along the way, and their statements were revealing:

- "I've never known so much about my church."
- "I know so much more now about ordained ministers, about the profession of ministry, and about being a lay minister."

1

- "Reading the breadth of views and expressions of faith on the part of the candidates was spiritually enriching."

Some of these respondents found that their friendship with the other church members of the committee deepened in new and rewarding ways:

"I saw our selfishness disappear during the process."
"I learned that nobody walks on water. . . . I could see a little of God in each of us. . . ."

I've heard those responses, too. Some people have said that serving on a search committee was a life-changing experience—one that brought about a quantum leap in faith development.

Time:
Committee
Work
Well, you know that something good has to be happening that would keep people working so hard in addition to what they usually do all day long. One of the committees on which I served met 11 times—approximately 45 hours over a six-month period. Another met 29 times for a total of at least 54 hours over a course of 18 months. Exactly two candidates were selected from more than 100 applicants. In both cases, committee members spent many hours studying written records about the candidates. Of the 37 people on these two committees, no one dropped out along the way, although I'm sure some were tempted. They stuck right to the job and expended an incredible amount of time and energy. I expect that such a time commitment is quite typical for most search committees, although the number of applicants for ordained ministerial positions may now be smaller.

So it's a big investment with tremendous rewards.
Yes, rewards in our understanding of our church and of ourselves, our own ministries. Every profile of an applicant is the story of a unique journey. When you read 50 or 60

stories of such personal and spiritual depth, your own spiritual journey moves forward in significant ways.

Then too, the search process brings limitless opportunities for personal growth. The job is very demanding. If you are not organized, you have to get organized. If you don't manage your time well, you have to learn to do it for this job. If you're a big talker, you've got to learn to be a big listener. If you're a silent thinker, you must learn to share your thoughts. You especially must learn to express a minority opinion, to speak succinctly, and to advocate persuasively.

Finally, people who have had this experience have spoken of a deep sense of accomplishment. One person told me of his joy in successfully discovering "the candidate": "Reaffirming the presence of the Holy Spirit in bringing us together is deeply moving and rewarding."

Let's go back to the beginning of the process. Do you think search committees ought to get some help with the process from outside the parish? And do you see some points in the process at which you think outside help is more important than others? I think it's useful for a person to see the search for a new ordained minister from a wide perspective. The task is very significant and yet its significance can be overestimated. The whole process of changing leadership starts when an ordained minister says to a key church member, "I'm going to be leaving." This announcement is sometimes months before a search committee is in place, and a good deal needs to happen to start the transfer of powers as smoothly as possible. The bond that has been forged between one clergyperson and one congregation must be broken with grace and bonding with a new pastor commenced. This bond will probably not be fully in place for at least a year after the new clergyperson arrives.

The success or failure of the new bond is affected by many other factors besides the actual selection of a successor.

PERSONAL AND
SPIRITUAL
REWARDS

STARTING OUT:
SEEKING HELP

When we look at failures, we find that some were affected by the state of the church well before the search process began. Perhaps a congregation did not attend to the grieving process that the Alban Institute has so well described, such as in Loren Mead's *Critical Moment of Ministry: A Change of Pastors* (a revised edition of which was issued in 2005 as *A Change of Pastors...And How It Affects Change in the Congregation*). Perhaps deep-seated conflict in the parish has gone unattended for years and therefore inundates and immobilizes a new pastor. Perhaps the tasks of relationship building in the critical first year of ministry are neglected. A search committee needs to realize that although its task is deeply significant in the life of the church, the congregation itself and its lay leaders have work to do from the first moment an ordained minister says, "I'm going to leave," through the first year or year and a half of the successor's ministry. Actions taken or not taken throughout this time span critically affect the success of the change to new leadership.

To return to your question of help in the search process, the most important source of assistance at the outset will be your church's judicatory [a generic term for your church's regional office, such as a diocese, conference, synod, or presbytery] office, which provides you with a clear outline of deployment expectations and practices in your region.

It's helpful to know that you have a real responsibility but your responsibility is not endless and total.

SELF-STUDY:
CHURCH
PROFILE

Yes, I think that principle is true and important for a search committee to understand. The committee members then are better able to address some of the predictable pitfalls in the search process that will make it more difficult for even the "perfect candidate" to become the "perfect minister" for a particular congregation. One of these is the self-study (or church profile) that the committee must write. The church *must* be described accurately. The difficulty of doing this task comes as a surprise to many search committee members. Its importance can hardly be overemphasized.

Again, if we learn from failures—those situations in which a matching of pastor to congregation did not survive the first 18 months—we might see that the view of reality presented to the candidate in the self-study (and later during a personal interview) turned out to be different from the realities the pastor faced upon arrival.

For instance, perhaps the ordained minister was told that the church wants to move toward more participatory or contemporary patterns of worship and then finds deep resistance to change in this area after being on the job for a period of time. Or perhaps the financial picture turns out to be far more complex than expected. The self-study is a critical part of the search process. It presents a picture of your church's history, its significant turning points, the challenges it now faces, its major accomplishments, the present patterns within its congregational life, and its goals and leadership needs.

Gathering data for the self-study is a challenging responsibility. One of the obvious mistakes a search committee must avoid is drawing the information for the self-study from too narrow a band in the congregational spectrum. Persons from all major organizations within the parish need to be asked for input through a variety of methods. Questionnaires, suggestion boxes, focus groups, conversations with lay leaders of the past, small-group meetings, and personal interviews with key people in the congregation are all possible ways of obtaining data. Analysis of this information certainly requires time and effort on the part of those people charged with the responsibility of writing the church profile; but the chances for reflecting an accurate and realistic picture of the church are greatly increased.

This document is as important to the committee itself as it is to judicatory persons who assist in the recruitment of candidates. Having reached a common understanding of your church's present life (including its history, current preoccupying issues, and hopes for the near future), you will not find it difficult to address its leadership needs and to begin to identify appropriate criteria for selecting your new pastor.

CRITERIA

Let me offer here a word of advice about these criteria. Taking time to define them in acceptable operational terms will save individual reading time and committee discussions later. Is "effective administrator" one of your criteria? An operational definition might be: "including, but not limited to, the candidate's ability to (1) support and supervise church staff; (2) provide overall attention to maintenance of church facilities; and (3) work supportively with governing boards." Are you looking for "flexibility"? This might be defined as "the degree to which candidate appears sensitive to many points of view and receptive to new ideas." Reaching agreement on what the criteria actually mean helps you select from the candidates' lengthy written records those experiences or recommendations that specifically relate to what you are looking for. With commonly understood criteria in place, you can use your hunches and intuition freely as you assess the candidates, knowing that these will reflect well the wide range of personal attitudes and opinions that probably exist in your congregation.

So it's really critically important that the search committee presents a picture of what is actually true in the church rather than a self-portrait that it *wishes* were true. Is the self-study another one of the points at which outside help is available?

RESOURCES

Yes, and the availability of such outside help is one of the first considerations of the committee. Because the judicatory head is a person who has had a tremendous amount of experience in the changing of church leadership, each judicatory has many resources. As a committee you'd want to invite him or her to be at your first meeting and to identify what role the judicatory expects to have in the search process. You'll need to know then of written resource material available to you, such as the valuable aids developed by the Alban Institute research [see the resource list] and the demographic information about your church community published by an agency such as Percept [Percept Group Inc.; http://www.perceptnet.com]. And certainly you'll need to consider use of a trained vacancy consultant; Alban senior consultant Roy Oswald has written some helpful information on this topic in his book *Beginning Ministry Together* [Alban, 2003].

For the parish that has been in conflict, with polarizing issues over a period of time, a skilled vacancy consultant is a resource of great value. In such cases, I would hope that the consultant would be brought into the situation at the earliest possible time, well before the search committee is formed, and stay with the parish through the first year of the new ministry. This does not mean that the consultant is at the church regularly but that his or her services are available to those who plan every important aspect of the transfer of leadership, from self-study to the eventual formation of a new relationship of pastor to parish. The costs of such services would be less than the risks involved in changing pastors during a time of turbulence without such help.

VACANCY CONSULTANTS

As an organization development consultant I certainly admit to some bias on this subject. I think a good consultant is enormously helpful in almost any circumstances, but I have to say in all honesty that I hope he or she is not actually needed. I like to think that transference of leadership in any organization is one of the essential powers it always possesses. It's the power to survive, to renew itself, to continue, to live on. This power must be within a healthy organization, not dependent upon outside help.

So this is not some weird, life-threatening crisis that has descended upon one's church. It is a part of an organization's life.

Exactly. Change of leadership is essentially a survival issue. I always hope that the ability to survive lies within an institution.

INTERIM
PASTORS

Under what conditions is it wise to have an interim pastor come in and give a parish special care for a period? It seems to me that this would be extremely important for a congregation enmeshed in conflict. An interim or acting pastor is important in almost any situation—when there has been a long and happy pastorate as well as when the situation has been turbulent. If the decision to obtain a pastoral interim has not already been made by the governing body, I would urge a search committee to focus attention on this matter during its first meeting. A trained interim minister can be an invaluable resource. If a congregation is not going to have one, is it prepared to maintain its own life and spirit for at least a year? I cannot imagine a church going through a responsible pastoral search in less than a year, and at the end of that time the new pastor will only just have been selected. It will probably be three months or more before he or she is actually on board. The search committee needs this time for its work and needs to be assured of responsible church leadership during this interval. Alban Institute research has clearly identified important developmental tasks of every parish during the interim period and helpful resources have been developed for use of lay leaders and search committee members.

If an acting or interim pastor is to be appointed, complete clarity is needed on the question of whether or not this person can be considered as a candidate for full-time pastor. The more effective he or she may be in performing pastoral duties in the interim, the more likely it is that members of the congregation will envision this temporary helper in the role of long-term leader. If there isn't clear agreement on how to handle this possibility at the outset, the entire congregation may experience pain.

That's very helpful. Let's move ahead then with this reasonably healthy congregation that has come to a predictable transition in its life. Maybe one of the

early questions would be the make-up of the search committee. What makes a good committee?

You should be aware of the extent to which you represent all factions of the congregation. Although the *size* of the committee will certainly have a bearing on the way it conducts its business, the *people* who are on it are of greater importance. If your church has a good deal of pluralism and diversity in its membership, it's essential that representatives of each subgroup are on the committee.

You will need to reexamine the generally accepted notion that the smaller the committee the better it will work. There are trade-offs to be made here. The smaller committee certainly has more opportunity for a free exchange of opinion during meetings. But think objectively of the advantages of the larger committee: it may represent more groups in the congregation; more of the needed skills for a successful search process are apt to be found in a larger group; and the sizeable amount of work can be better shared. If you expect 50 candidates for the position of pastor, 12 people can more easily divide the task of reading the applications than can six or eight people. Considering the inescapable fact that everyone volunteers to do this job on top of a full day's activity, sharing the sizeable amount of work is not unimportant.

The disadvantage of the large committee is that it requires highly disciplined meetings, which must be accomplished either by its leader or, hopefully, through a growing self-discipline on the part of the members. Learning to work as a large team is difficult. You need to remind yourselves frequently that your participation in this task is an act of faith. Sharing your images, apprehensions, expectations, and hopes will take longer. But my guess is that if your large committee is truly representative of a diverse congregation, your work together on this task will have a greater chance of being personally rewarding as well as institutionally beneficial.

COMMITTEE
MEMBERSHIP
AND SIZE

You are underlining for me the importance of a search committee paying attention to getting itself formed into a working team. Are there some special things that this committee can do to help bring that about?

FIRST STEPS   Well, this will probably be started in the second meeting. The best *first step* in team building is to agree that you are not going to allow yourselves to be rushed. I think all of us tend to approach our volunteer work in a relatively well-organized manner, ready to get down to business right away. I'm not knocking that. No one wants to waste time in their volunteer work any more than in their daily work. But once having determined a reasonable amount of time for the search process in your church and having made necessary decisions about resources available to you through your judicatory, your most important task is to know yourselves, and this task takes time. The problem is that getting to know one another can be embarrassing, unless your church is very small and intimate. You probably are all vaguely familiar with each other. You know where you usually sit in church, and you may even know each other's name. Yet, somehow during the coffee hours you haven't asked, "What do you do from Monday to Saturday?" You may not know each other's interests, skills, and available time. Where do you live? When are you going to be able to meet? These are mundane questions but the answers are necessary to get this team working together.

VISIONS AND   What's your vision of what our new minister will look
SECRETS   like? That's a profound question. It's also a secret that every person on the search committee holds. The sooner this secret is shared, the better. Moreover, most persons have a fear of something the committee might or might not do:

- "Penelope will probably dominate every meeting and none of us will be able to get a word in edgewise . . ."
- "These young folks will probably call a gay minister and my mother will leave the church . . ."

Fears such as these may strongly affect a person's behavior and hence the committee's progress. A wise committee chair takes steps in the beginning to build a climate of trust where members feel comfortable to share fears that are related to the search process.

Finally, all people have activities they like to be engaged in and activities they are good at. In the course of the search you will need many kinds of skills, and if they are not found within the committee, they must be contracted for from outside. Sharing your skills, experiences, and gifts is an important step to take as you get to know one another and what you bring to this job.

So my advice is: resist your commendable urges to get organized fast, choose your leader, and get on with the job. First, spend some time on learning who you are and what you bring to this task.

What you just said sounds to me like an outline for that getting-on-board process. People might take those very questions and work with them for a while. They will not be wasting time if they spend a meeting on themselves as resources to the search process and on this task as a ministry, the beginning of a journey that has great possibilities for personal and spiritual growth as well as a very specific and valuable end product. When you recognize that you are going to be spending a lot of time together on a journey, you are willing to take time at the start to deepen the knowledge you have of each other—knowledge which, if it has developed by sitting across the aisle for years, may be scant.

GETTING ON
BOARD
TOGETHER

Well, I can see some of the pitfalls may be related to the failure to do that getting-on-board work. If your secret hopes for ordained leadership are not shared, I can imagine the troubles that might come later when people operate out of these hidden fantasies. I can also imagine committee members saying, "Gosh, I wish we had known that Joe was so good at this

and Mary really had all this background in interviewing."

Getting to know each other doesn't take very long, and it's not done "once and for all." You're just making a start at knowing each other, what you bring to this task, what some of your visions are. This is a demanding job. The organizing tasks of the self-study, for example, are formidable. It's best to know where your troops are, what skills and energy are on hand. Then you can move with speed and effectiveness.

Do you have some specific suggestions about all the many tasks that lie ahead for this committee? How do you decide who is going to do what?

NECESSARY SKILLS

Those decisions become easier when you know something of who you are as individuals. The job requires persons with many gifts. No list will be complete. I suspect your committee will need people who have skills and experience in such areas as: overall project management, leading meetings, writing, editing, designing questionnaires, public speaking, interviewing, organizing office routines—and the list could go on. As you are going around the circle of your committee for the first time and someone mumbles that he or she is a computer expert or statistician, rejoice! That's a big help. Someone who works in career development will probably be helpful as interviewing time approaches. Celebrate the person who is experienced and willing to keep track of a great deal of paperwork in an effective office system. Celebrate also the persons who volunteer to write letters that convey clear messages in caring and compassionate terms. You may need two or three people like that.

In addition to these skills, there are personal attributes that will be useful to the work of this committee. You will need people who will be advocates, who are not worried about expressing a minority opinion. You will need persons who have many friends in the congregation but who at the same time can accept the discomfort of maintaining confidentiality. As I mentioned earlier, you will need persons who are willing to do considerably more listening than speaking during your meetings . . . or at the least, people who are willing to learn to do that!

You're scaring me a little bit! It sounds as though you are drawing a picture of a very high-powered group formed of professional statisticians, and I find myself thinking "Whoa, we don't have any fancy people like that in our church. But, we may well have some people who use the skills you're talking about in different ways."

You're right! I don't mean to imply that a search committee requires specialists. The point is that you say to yourselves, "These are the tasks to be done and here are the skills we'll need. If we don't have these skills ourselves, we must either learn them or beg, borrow, or buy them from outside our group."

Five key tasks need to be done: (1) describe your church (the church profile); (2) determine the criteria for choosing your new ordained minister; (3) evaluate your candidates from their written records; (4) select promising candidates from personal contact; and (5) present the best candidate(s) to your church or its leaders. These tasks sound simple, but each one contains its challenges and human dilemmas.

Your choice of committee chairperson is particularly important. Certainly it helps to have someone who is widely respected by your congregation. Regardless of how smoothly the search process goes, there is bound to be a degree of tension, if not anxiety, in a parish during this transitional period. Your leader can reassure the congregation both formally during the service and informally through a variety of church activities if he or she is a person known and trusted widely in the congregation. In addition, you should choose as your leader a person experienced and skilled in leading meetings. You need a chairperson who is used to working under pressures of time, who can follow a

SEARCH
COMMITTEE
TASKS

COMMITTEE
LEADERSHIP

clear agenda towards an agreed-on purpose, and who is able to manage the meetings so that all members of the committee contribute. My experience leads me to advise you to *assume* that this person is already too busy! You will need to assure him or her that you will relieve him of every possible task other than overall committee leadership and meeting management; then you must work diligently to keep this promise.

Could you say a little bit more about the vital task of helping the congregation come to the point where they can say goodbye to the pastor who is leaving and thus be free to move on to a new person who will be very different? Do you have any words of wisdom to the committee about how to help themselves and the congregation do that?

SAYING GOODBYE

I hope that the whole church is doing some ceremonial grieving. It needs to be done, and it requires time. The search committee will be aided in handling its own separation issues if it can arrange to hold an exit interview with the pastor and spouse who will be able to provide you with information about your church that you could not hear from anyone else. The ordained minister (and family) sees the realities of church life from a unique point of view. You probably will gain a deeper understanding of patterns in your church life that will strengthen your self-study. The exit interview itself is often a freeing and satisfying experience for all involved.

Saying good-bye may still be a problem even in a normally happy situation. It takes a while before you will be able to look at the needs of your church without seeing in those needs a reflection of the inadequacies of your — former pastor. As you talk more and more openly to each other, you learn a great deal more about your ordained minister and about your church than you now know. The actual reading of so many applications during the early screening process helps you focus on new possibilities and worry less about strengths and weaknesses of your previous pastor.

A whole breadth of possibilities are opening up that we might not have thought of before, as we begin to look at all these different candidates with their different strengths.
Right. You see how other clergy have worked in a variety of churches. Separation may continue to be worrisome, but sooner or later the experience becomes less of a problem as you find yourself having to suffer that separation from many good candidates whom you've met on paper or in personal interviews. Your faith is being renewed over and over by seeing so many ways in which clergy are performing ministry.

As the committee begins to move into this stage of corresponding with and interviewing candidates, what have you experienced as some of the tricky places in that process?
Let's separate the stages of the process. In the first stage, you know the candidate from his or her written record. In the second, your knowledge comes from personal contact. I think one of the shocks occurs when you discover how the actual person differs from the image you have formed through the written word. This is a time for reassurance. Your initial reading of a large group of applicant records enables you to evaluate each candidate according to criteria derived through the self-study of your church. With little difficulty, you can identify a small group who appear at first reading to be outstanding candidates, a small group who appear unsuitable for a variety of reasons, and a sizeable group about whom there is either a difference of opinion or insufficient information. You get additional written material—such as written answers to questions you ask, copies of sermons, reactions to your self-study—and hold telephone conversations with references. But when

STAGES OF
THE PROCESS

members of a committee go to see and hear a candidate, or one comes for a group interview, you find that the image the committee has of this person is totally different from the reality. Self-doubt strikes with force. "What are we doing here?" "Have we been wasting time studying all these records?"

SCREENING
PROCESSES

Let me say something about self-doubt and its first cousin, guilt. It is expressed in many ways. Screening out applicants for any sought-after position is an acutely uncomfortable job. In a voluntary organization, I suspect that no matter how fair the procedure you devise or how clear the criteria, you feel uncomfortable doing it. In a church-related selection process, you feel guilty, particularly if you use some sort of numerical rating system to screen candidates. I have heard committee members say, "It just doesn't seem fair to give a numerical rating to a person, especially not an ordained minister. I haven't read enough. I don't know enough. I haven't seen enough. I spent only 20 minutes reading that profile."

Now is a time to look at the facts and reassure each other. Now is the time for being reminded of your purpose and the acts of faith you are jointly involved in. Your 20-minute reading may seem inadequate for eliminating a serious candidate from further consideration by your committee. But it is not really inadequate. If even 10 members of the committee have spent 20 minutes each in reviewing the written record of a candidate, that person has received more than three hours of study. Although you may be working from a common set of criteria, all 10 of you are seeing different aspects of the candidate in the written record. You do not need to fear that any important strength—or weakness—has been overlooked by so many people. Trust your judgment. Trust the judgment of the other committee members. Trust the process. If after honest exchange of different views, the consensus is that a candidate does not appear to be right for your church, allow yourselves to take this action without guilt.

I would think that a lot of the guilt might come from a preconception that the process is completely rational. But my perception is that the process has some rational steps, but it is also a more than rational process that includes going with your hunches, a process of discernment.

Yes, discernment and trust. I think you will find that if the meetings are focused with some form of worship, you affirm that you are open to the Holy Spirit in your work. You acknowledge that your powers are limited, that you are going to put your best efforts into your search for a new ordained minister but that, through you, another plan is being worked out. It's helpful to close the meetings in worship as well, for in this way you'll recognize some of the ways that the Holy Spirit has been working through you during your time together.

SPIRITUAL GROUNDING

You mentioned using numerical rating scales earlier. Could you say more about these?

I've noted that a good deal of ambivalence seems to crop up among committee members when rating instruments are designed and used. In the initial stages of screening candidates, however, rating scales derived from criteria can be very useful to a diverse group of people reading lengthy profiles. When you share your individual ratings of the candidates, your committee will see the three groups of candidates I spoke of earlier very clearly and far more quickly than discussing the list one by one: the small top group, the small bottom group, and the large group in the middle who present an unclear picture. Your ratings can be used to identify persons in this large group who impress individual committee members quite differently. Let's say you are using a numerical scale where candidates are rated on various criteria on a range from 0 to 100. When you have several candidates, for example, whom six persons on the committee rate high in the 70s and five persons rate in the 40s on particular criteria, you know quickly where to direct your

RATING SCALES AND RANKINGS

attention. Sometimes this can lead to an important reconsideration of your criteria. What exactly do we mean when we say we want a "good administrator?" How are we defining "urban sensitivity?" What are the signs in the written record of a good preacher? So the discipline of individually rating an applicant according to agreed-upon criteria can result in quick agreement on some candidates and a healthy discussion of your basic criteria as these apply to others.

When the time comes for selection of a small group of top candidates with whom to have personal contact, I believe that ratings are no longer appropriate. At this stage, members of the committee should be asked to rank the candidates in the order of their preference. I would hope that by this time every one of the top candidates would have been supported by an articulate and persuasive group of advocates, that people have had a chance to express concerns, and that a specific amount of time has been spent in discussing each candidate. At this point if each person takes time in silence to place the candidates in order of preference and to share these rankings without discussion, the will of the group can be quickly discerned. This very helpful process may reveal a clear and compelling consensus among you. If so, celebrate!

That sounds exciting! But I'd like to back up for a minute. It seems to me that the kinds of secrets that people might bring to the committee, the kinds of pictures they may have in their mind, and the kinds of assumptions they may have about the ordained leadership that is waiting for them out there in the future, may fail to include some variations in sex, race, age, or sexual orientation. Some important possibilities for their future may be prematurely foreclosed by those assumptions. What helps members of the committee open up their minds to look at something that may not be traditional for their church?

I can think of three actions that can help: (1) sharing the inner vision of what the new minister might look like that each person brings to the search; (2) learning the realities about clergy supply in your denomination; and (3) clarifying the distinction between affirmative action and equal opportunity procedures.

NONTRADITIONAL CANDIDATES

Even if no surprises occur from the first process of screening profiles, a brief description of the ministry as a profession may expand the possibilities in the minds of some search committee members. I did not know, for example, that in 2004 the United Church of Christ had more than 2,500 active ordained women clergy, comprising 27 percent of their clergy roster, and that there are more women in its seminaries than men. Nor did I know that in the Washington, D.C., area more ordained clergy are presently in secular jobs than in parishes. This has a profound effect on placement patterns. So I advise a committee to find the answers to these questions: Who are the clergy now? What are they doing? What are their spouses doing? Current information is a good antidote to stereotyping. Your judicatory head can tell you these "facts of clergy life."

Finally, it is important to be clear about your committee goals as these relate to a different kind of leader than you're used to. Search committees of some organizations work under an affirmative action mandate to attract more women, minorities, or handicapped persons into positions of leadership. The goals of other committees assure that these groups are given an equal opportunity to seek the position. Selection is then made on the basis of merit. The two policies require very different action steps to support them, which are often confused. A policy of affirmative action is going to result in a careful analysis of required skill and training for each position, with agreement on what aspects can be developed on the job. Equal opportunity refers to information about a job opening and access to it; selection from a broad base of candidates is made on merit. Your church search committee needs to be clear about how these

AFFIRMATIVE ACTION AND EQUAL OPPORTUNITY

issues affect both the thinking of individual members and the intended work of the committee as a whole.

The question of the wide variety of clergy available deserves a good deal of thought. Your committee may receive profiles from unmarried ministers, from persons who have been or are going through a divorce, from clergy couples seeking to share a pastorate, from ministers trained and experienced in your denomination's traditions outside of North America, from ministers under 30 or over 60, from openly gay pastors, from persons of color, or from two-career couples—all of whom may represent a departure from what you expected. When these persons come up for review and discussion, you need to take the time to share your experience, your hopes, your hunches, your fears.

Get your feelings out on the table.

And that is never done once and for all, never. You need to become more and more open with each other as these candidates come up for consideration. Take each situation as an opportunity to broaden your personal vision of your church's new pastor. Suppose, for example, that one of the first promising candidates you consider as a committee is a unmarried, ordained male. Take the time on the spot to share your thoughts about matching a single male to your church. What gifts might this person bring to your congregation? What concerns might need to be addressed? How might your church change under his ministry? What aspects might remain the same? Who might be affected by the presence of a single minister and how? Taking the time to share your individual assumptions about a promising candidate who is unmarried and any related fears or concerns that individual committee members may have will strengthen your trust in each other and ultimately your ability to discern God's will as it is working through your search committee.

Also, at this time a sentence that begins, "I don't think our church is ready for . . ." is *not* helpful. The reason that we often hear this phrase is understandable: in an uncomfortable crunch time it is much easier to talk in terms of "they" in the church rather than "we" on the committee. The sooner your committee can think, talk, and act as the church, the better. Members of a committee need to develop the degree of trust in each other that helps one person say to another: "I sense your concern. Can you state it in your own terms rather than as 'they' might see it?" This allows you to acknowledge your own apprehensions as well as your hopes. When you trust each other, you can worry out loud.

Now you're speaking about the burden of authority that this group has been given and the responsibility they have to own that authority, even when it gets uncomfortable—which it will.

I suspect that any church that calls its first woman pastor or a person of a different race than the majority of the congregation will need to do a good deal of additional work and praying to make this new venture a success. In the case of the excellent but different candidate, it is better to try to understand just what these tasks might be than to dismiss the opportunity with "Our church is not ready for . . ."

That's very helpful, the way you put it. We are beginning now to move into a stage in the process where we see a real person emerging out of the future. I can imagine that one of the difficulties the members of a search committee may face is that they are so conscious of the importance of their task and the needs of their church that they get exclusively focused in on those concerns, failing to notice that they are encountering some real human beings. I wonder whether you've found some ways committees can be conscious of the needs of that other person.

If you have 45 candidates, you are ultimately going to reject 44 of them. How this task is done—the quality of your

CARING
COMMUNICATION

relationship with all these people—is primary. The whole committee needs to be concerned. But I think that usually you will find two or three persons on the committee who are willing to act as ombudsmen for the 44, accepting the responsibility of responding to their applications quickly and communicating the committee's decisions in both clear and compassionate words. This caring is more difficult than it sounds, for this is not a tidy, businesslike procedure. The names of candidates do not come in at one time through one channel. Since you will often have calls or letters about a candidate who does not know that he or she is under consideration, your letter writers must initiate some of the correspondence. This job is not easy and extends over the entire course of the search. Therefore, rather than one lone correspondence secretary, I would recommend that you ask a small group to assume this burden, charging them with the responsibility of seeing this through the eyes and hearts of candidates who, for a time, are relating to your church in a deeply significant and personal way, and who deserve your Christian consideration. Your letter writers may easily find phraseology that is appropriate to many candidates. The fact remains that each recipient is more apt to receive a prompt and personal reply if one person has taken the time to look carefully at the candidate's written records.

Communication with the much smaller group of people remaining under consideration becomes more specific. You want more information from them. They want to know a great deal about you. Your letters should be direct and honest: "You remain under consideration. We would like to know more about you. We enclose a copy of the self-study that we have made so that you will know as much about us as possible. As you read it, think of experiences in your ministry that might be particularly useful if you were to become our pastor. We would like to talk to people who know you. We would like copies or tapes of sermons you think would be appropriate for our church. After we receive your material, you can expect to hear further from us in approximately _____."

Having studied this additional information, the sooner you meet your top candidates in person the better. Establish personal contact by telephone. Arrange a mutually convenient time and place and confirm all plans in writing. Try to have as many committee members as possible be with the candidate during the informal hours of the visit. When scheduling the interview with the entire committee, be aware of the kind of day your candidate has had and be sensitive to needs for rest and food.

And finally you will come to the exciting point of identifying from this group those two or three who, although they may be totally different in appearance, style, and/or experience, all have the promise of matching your situation in such a way that a new and vigorous church can emerge under their leadership. You go ahead and rank them: you're going to ask this one first, then the next one second, and the other you will ask third. They are all different. They are all outstanding. Your church can thrive with each person but in different ways. You must rank them.

RANKING
YOUR CHOICES

There are no other options.

No, and at this stage, your chairperson must communicate with each one with the greatest possible honesty and care. Assume that all three candidates are mature adults who have dealt with success and rejection in their ministerial careers, have also made hard decisions involving other people, and have experienced both joy and disappointment in their work. After the committee has reached consensus on the order in which the top candidates will be called, all three deserve to be informed by telephone or in person as promptly and as thoughtfully as possible. No need exists here for advising you about communicating with your top candidate—let your heart lead. But a clear and truthful conversation with the other two is absolutely essential. "We have been studying for over a year now and you are among the top three of the 45 candidates for our pastor. At the same time, we need to tell you in all honesty that we are in serious discussion with another pastor. We will keep in touch with you by telephone as the results of these discussions become clear. . . ."

You must realize that your first choice among the candidates may find compelling reasons to remain in his or her present work or to accept another call. A continuing relationship based on integrity and concern with the other two is vital until a new covenant has been forged.

Talking about this stage in the process reminds me that confidentiality is one of the issues with which committee members will be dealing. What are the areas in which this concern is really important?

CONFIDENTIALITY   Maintaining confidentiality is one of the sources of human stress that you as a search committee member can predict with certainty. There's no way to avoid it. The strains can be lessened, however, if you use every available opportunity to inform the congregation of what you are doing at each stage of the search process. By all means, use a multimedia approach! Notices on a bulletin board, brief summaries from the chairperson during pulpit announcements, articles in your church newsletter, special letters or e-mails to the congregation—each method brings your message to an increasingly large part of your church membership: "We are organized. We are on our way in the search process. In the next two months we will be studying our church in order that we can accurately describe ourselves to our candidates. We will need your help in this task, and some of the ways we are going to include you are . . . [for instance, meetings, surveys, small-group discussions, *focus groups*]. During this time we want every suggestion you can give us on the choosing of our new minister, including names of promising candidates. After the self-study has been completed, we will be screening candidates from their written records. At this time, we would not be fair to our candidates if we were to discuss them at all." This message will probably have to be stated in some manner at least every month and, even then, will not eliminate the very real and well-intentioned curiosity and apprehension felt by many members of a congregation at the time of pastoral change.

It is helpful to allow time at the start of each meeting for people to share problems that may have arisen for them from their role on the search committee. "What's been happening since we last met?" "What can we say when we've been asked whether a particular minister has been interviewed?" "I didn't know how to answer when one of my friends told me after church last Sunday that she heard that we are considering a woman for our minister and she doesn't think that is a good idea." "A lot of people have been telling me that we ought to be considering our interim minister—his sermons have been so good." My point is that the role of search committee members is not always going to be comfortable. You need to acknowledge this in your meetings by providing time in a busy agenda for your own group care and support.

COMMITTEE
CHALLENGES

You told me earlier that members of the committee will experience despair, guilt, and anger as well as accomplishment, pride, and joy. Now you're talking about one of the rough spots.

It certainly is. We're all vulnerable. This time is one of uncertainty. A church can live a long time without formal leadership, but only if it manages in some way the stress that everyone experiences during this transition. The Alban Institute has done valuable research on what needs to happen between ministers, identifying the necessary developmental tasks and landmarks between termination of one ministry and start-up of a successor.

LIVING WITH
UNCERTAINTY

Renewal and vigor depend on lay leaders paying attention to each landmark in the transition process. I think I've indicated other points along the way at which search committee members may experience discomfort and would appreciate support. Certainly members can feel real pangs of despair during the initial screening phase when the complexity of the job becomes apparent. You may begin to lose confidence in yourself or the committee. You begin to doubt whether you have the time to do a conscientious job of reviewing each candidate. As the need for confidentiality begins to affect your normal patterns of relating to your fellow parishioners (to say nothing of your spouse!), your feelings about the role you have assumed in your church can become tinged with anger and confusion. When a promising candidate withdraws his/her name from further consideration, you tend to feel rejected. Such feelings need to be surfaced and shared in your committee meetings. You need to be reassured that you have what it takes to serve your church in this special way. What you are doing is indeed a valuable ministry.

There's an important religious question here, isn't there? Committee members need to be working all the time to understand that their responsibility is real but not ultimate, and what is being laid on them is not so much being *successful* as being *faithful* in their task. Those uncomfortable feelings come from living in faith, not a false certainty.

PERSONAL
SUPPORT

Yes, faith is very much the issue. If you affirm quickly in the midst of the process that you are on a journey, you perhaps can see more easily how far forward you have in fact moved. Keep in touch with the degree to which you have been rewarded. One hard-working member of a search committee said to me, "I was ready to quit. Reading all those profiles and having differing opinions from the other committee members gave me a different vision of what kind of person will be needed. I realized that we were supposed to be about a third of the way through the job and it's bigger than we ever imagined it would be. How will this diverse group of people ever be able to come together on one person?"

But as committee members find more ways to be supportive to each other and as they work and worship together, it slowly begins to happen. Commitment to the task deepens, trust in each other increases, and self-confidence is reaffirmed. You may experience significant growth in your own personal faith.

From what you are saying, it sounds as though it would be important for the committee to look back on its journey at the end, to celebrate, to laugh over some of the funny times, to remember some of the rough times and to hold up some of the gifts from this journey together.

It's important to do that in the middle as well as at the end! As a matter of fact, I think it's important for the committee to give itself permission to laugh a lot right from the start of this stressful process. Humor helps. Start a collection of all those ridiculous rating scales about picking ministers. Half of them were written by ministers themselves as they strive to ease the tensions around new placement. Have you seen the one about picking your minister the way you do a new car? It's great.

CELEBRATING TOGETHER

Take some time off together. Meet in a different place. Have a potluck supper. Search committee meetings can be long. On one of my recent experiences, our work was completed during 11 meetings in six months. Because members traveled long distances to attend, the meetings were from three to eight hours long. One evening the electricity went off in our meeting space. We all moved to the home of one of the members and continued through our agenda. But that small experience increased our understanding and enjoyment of each other. A task with some built-in difficulties became less stressful for us all.

I guess what I'm saying is pay attention to your process. Those human feelings that you are experiencing of joy or anger, confidence or despair, curiosity about each other, or anxiety about the task—they need to be dealt with openly in your work together. They are a legitimate part of a well-planned search committee agenda. If informal occasions can be arranged, however, the need for such time during the meetings themselves may be lessened but not eliminated.

WORK AND
MEETING
SPACE

Speaking of taking care of yourselves reminds me of the seemingly mundane question of your meeting space. It's really very important. You are working together over a long period of time. You need a comfortable, secure room in the church with enough space for keeping committee files as well as a large meeting table and chairs. Ask for the loan of one or two easy chairs and a good reading lamp for committee members who stop by the church for an hour of two of reading. Erect a graffiti board to chronicle what you've been running into along the way. See if the church can provide you with a computer on which you can keep all electronic files related to the search process and compose letters and e-mails to candidates and others involved in the process. Ask for the loan of a cassette-tape deck, VCR, or DVD player, so that when you receive tapes or disks of sermons, these can be reviewed by a group of committee members together in your meeting room. If your church does not provide you with a comfortable and secure place in which to study the written records, these then must be circulated among committee members, which is more difficult, time consuming, and expensive.

Committee comfort and confidentiality are not superficial matters. I urge you to consider your committee surroundings carefully at the start of your work together. A room of your own—you will need it to meet, to read, to listen, to discuss, to record, to write letters, to file, to interview, to make hard decisions, and to plan how best to carry out your decisions. As your committee ends its journey together, you can dismantle the room. That experience can be a part of closure.

I know that you value the church's ability to manage changes in leadership as one of the natural, ongoing, unfolding stages of its life. I suppose you'd say that

that capacity is one of the things a church will have at the end of the road, when this committee has managed its tasks well. Having experienced that capacity will be one of the payoffs for the church.

It certainly is a payoff for the church, but not one that we tend to notice. How many of us recognize, for example, the smooth transition of leadership that we usually experience in the United States between presidents? Most of us find ourselves so engaged in the intensity and drama of a national election that we fail to celebrate our country's extraordinary capacity to transfer power at the highest level of government in a peaceful manner. The same truth can be said in any institution. In the face of so many decisions, hopes, fears, questions, and uncertainties, a congregation, not surprisingly, loses track of the inevitability of pastoral change. We tend to resist rather than accept what we rightly describe as a natural, ongoing stage of church life.

The search committee itself needs to recognize and celebrate its accomplishments all along the journey. For a time you become a church within a church, a group of people gathered together to discern how the Holy Spirit can work through you. When you first are aware of a strong consensus among your diverse group, you are exhilarated. When you see yourselves as a group of people who have moved from working together haphazardly, or even at cross-purposes, to a pattern of effective and satisfying collaboration, you are exhilarated. When you have conducted a successful group interview, you are exhilarated. When you present your candidate to your congregation in what is perceived as an act of worship, you are exhilarated. Four good reasons for celebration right there!

Could you say more about a group interview—what makes that a desirable process and what can help ensure their success?

In a sense the interview is a final test of a committee's ability to work together effectively. Two or three committee

HIGH POINTS

GROUP
INTERVIEWS

members interviewing a candidate is a far easier technique than having the whole group conduct the interview. Once a small group has interviewed the candidate, however, its members then have the burden of transferring their perceptions to the rest of the committee. Something is lost in the transference. More is lost through the human tendency to listen and remember selectively. Sooner or later the entire committee needs to talk with a serious candidate face-to-face. I urge that you do this interview with the whole committee as soon as possible.

Group interviews are likely to be successful if they are carefully planned in a meeting devoted entirely to this purpose. The time you expect to take in the interview is an important committee decision. I feel strongly that an interview lasting more than two hours is an imposition on any person. Any interview can be successfully accomplished in an hour and a half if the time is well spent.

PLANNING THE
INTERVIEW

This time period is valuable. How should it be used? You agree first upon exactly what needs to be told to the visitor during this time. This task is more difficult than it sounds, as a great deal of conversation may be interesting and informative but more appropriately brought up at a later date. What, then, are the questions that you as a committee want to ask all candidates? What are the questions you have about this particular candidate? What aspects of his or her ministry have given you puzzling or contradictory messages? Who will ask these questions? When, during the hour and a half, will you provide time for the candidate to respond to your self-study? To give you his or her reasons for being interested in your church? To ask *you* questions? How do you wish to close the interview? Who will do this? Do not fear that an interview so carefully planned will seem uncomfortably controlled and structured. The opposite is more likely to be true: without an agreed-upon game plan, a committee can easily find that unimportant conversations can dominate the time, leaving both interviewers and interviewee with the frustrating feeling that much of importance was not addressed.

Your interview plan, finally, should include time after the candidate has left for individual note-taking on the part of the entire committee. This time is not for entering into a heated discussion of the strengths or weaknesses that you have observed. Your impressions of the candidate are valid, important, and need to be recorded. If you are interviewing several persons over the course of several weeks, committee members must have accurate notes of clear and significant impressions of each candidate when the committee holds its final decision-making sessions. These perceptions are easier to forget than you may realize. Resist the urge to discuss the candidate before jotting down your thoughts.

I think you can see why I feel that the search committee that conducts a series of group interviews with success and satisfaction has much to celebrate. Although this work requires careful preparation and self-discipline on the part of the committee members, the chances are that all parties may view the experience as personally and professionally rewarding.

In addition to the group interview, I urge you to ask every serious candidate for your church to lead the search committee in worship at some time during his or her visit to your parish. Worshiping together provides you and your candidate an invaluable glimpse into the possibilities of new ministry together. It is the essential action that affirms that what you are doing is *calling* rather than *hiring* a new pastor.

Well, those are the questions I wanted to ask you. Did we leave out something essential?

We need to look carefully at the search committee's primary task: choosing a pastor to recommend to the congregation. Once a committee has completed the group interviews, worshiped with the candidates, checked their references, and considered their individual gifts for your congregation, its members meet to make their final decision on a person or persons to recommend to their congregation. The way of making this decision is called *discernment,* one of the most

DISCERNMENT

misunderstood concepts in church leadership. Discernment is the process whereby a group strives to understand what God is calling the group to do. It is also the process that an individual pastor goes through in determining whether God is calling him or her to accept a call to a particular parish.

I think of discernment as "consensus with prayer." In the case of a group, it is not necessarily unanimity. An individual may think along these lines: "I understand what most of you would like to do and personally I would not choose that path. But I feel that you have heard and understood my alternative. I have had sufficient opportunity to sway you to my point of view and have not been able to do so. So I will gladly go along with what most of us want to do ..."

Discernment succeeds only when members of a group have an intense desire both to *do* God's will as well as to *know* it. After having spent hours and months together in the search for a new pastor for your congregation, you are certainly ready for action! First, committee members share with the group their individual thoughts and feelings about the candidate under consideration. Then, putting resumés, profiles, and rating scales aside, the committee takes time in individual reflection and prayer: What might our church be like under this person's spiritual leadership? How might we as a congregation grow? How might I find new avenues of lay ministry? What issues would we need to face as a congregation in calling this person to ministry with us? And finally, the ultimate question for each member to answer for himself or herself: should our church call this person—yes or no?

REACHING
CONSENSUS

After prayer by the whole group, each member states *yes* or *no* without further elaboration. Is there consensus? Is there now a clear direction that the committee is going? Can the entire search committee see this as God's will? If so, rejoice!

If not, continue the discernment cycle: share as a group your additional thoughts, feelings, concerns, fears, hopes and expectations about the candidate, pray; answer for yourself, "From what I have learned in further reflection and from my colleagues on this committee, should our church call this person?" Report your individual conclusion to the group; check again for consensus.

Obviously discernment, like consensus, can be time consuming. Everyone in the group must be willing to take the necessary time. The danger is that if you rush, you risk thinking that *your* will is God's will. Discernment is trying to decide what God wants *your group* to do. In addition to time, it requires complete trust in the sincerity of others in the group and an unwavering belief that each person's views count in finding the truth.

Decisions made by consensus and discernment tend to have higher commitment than decisions made by vote, especially close votes where there are definite winners and losers. For instance, where church by-laws require a vote on formal board action, this procedure best takes place after consensus has been reached.

Finally, once your committee has discerned the best candidate(s) for your new minister, and when an agreement has been negotiated with a candidate, the congregation and its lay leaders must be informed. Whatever procedural requirements various denominations may have, I would hope that the search committee itself would take the major role in this task. You are the people who have struggled through the months to ascertain the needs of your church. You are the people who, after hours of consideration of different examples of ministerial style, experience, words and actions, have formed a vision of your church as it might look under the leadership of a particular ordained minister. Your vision needs to be shared at the time of first disclosure of your candidate to church leaders and to the congregation—not what he or she *looks* like but what your church as a community of faith might *be* like with his or her leadership. Such a presentation becomes then an act of worship in itself—a church in action, faith in action, and

PRESENTATION OF CANDIDATE

the promise of new *congregational* life. This experience can
be the most deeply rewarding moment in the life of the
search committee—the end of one church, the beginning
of the new.

As I say this, I realize that I am back where I started,
thinking about the personal rewards of accepting the job
of membership on a search committee. Early in the process
you asked, first silently, then openly, "Why am I doing this?"
You probably didn't know how much work you were
getting into. Ask yourself again, "Why am I doing this?" I
think the answer gets right down to the nature of our
relationship to our church. In volunteering to serve in this
capacity we are pushed back against our own priorities. We
progress from "Why am I doing this?" to "Why am I at
church?" to "What is church to me? What is ministry?" For
me it's just three simple relationships: ministry has to do
with how I relate to God, how I relate to you, and how a
church relates to its community. It means the professional
ministry and the lay ministry, both together, both separate,
influencing and empowering the other. Participation in the
search process rewards us by increasing our understanding
of all dimensions of ministry. In so doing, our faith is tested
and deepened. We grow. We change. And I believe that this
is why we come to church: to have our faith deepened, to
grow, to change. Each of us is seeking to discover truth.
Participation in the search for a new ordained minister tends
to hasten that discovery.

**Serving on a search committee is a great opportunity
to grow up in our faith. During the ordinary passage
of the years that preceded this activity, people may
have come to feel that the ordained minister is really
running the church and that people can just get
comfortably dependent upon that leadership.
Searching for new ordained leadership is a time when
the laity can come to have an important sense of
"this is my church."**

You're absolutely right, and the laity also become aware that the building of their relationship with a new minister means the building of a new church. Some aspects of the church that have been in place for many years will continue regardless of who the new pastor is. But at the same time, the church will never be the same again. A new covenant is born, and therefore a new church is given birth. After the work of the search committee is over, new tasks arise to forge the new covenant between pastor and people. Power within the congregation has probably been at least jostled, if not actually shifted, during the interim period and will need to be reestablished along new lines. Although individual members may be called upon to assume specific roles in support of the new pastor, a formal role for the search committee in the forging of the new covenant does not exist. That group's work is completed with the primary announcement: "We recommend this person to you as your ordained minister because we think that you and [s]he will make the strongest ministerial team our church can have at this time." The relationship between congregation and new pastor then gets bonded both formally and informally over the next year or so. Through their increased understanding of the church and its ministry, individual committee members have the power to help that bonding take place. The responsibility for doing this bonding, however, rests fully on the entire congregation, its new lay leaders, and the new pastor. They must learn to know and to trust each other in yet another cycle in the life of the church.

A NEW CHURCH

BIBLIOGRAPHY

The Alban Institute has probably produced more helpful resources for congregations undergoing pastoral transitions than other publisher or organization. As his multiple titles listed here indicate, the work of Alban senior consultant Roy Oswald has particularly helped to define this field. The titles described below do not exhaust the resources that congregations and their leaders might find useful in navigating pastoral transitions, from Alban or otherwise, but do represent a core library of publications that address the key issues. For additional resources on pastoral transitions, we recommend that you visit the Congregational Resource Guide Web site (http://www.congregationalresources.org), which provides annotated listings of many more publications, organizations, and resources that will be helpful as you meet this critical moment of ministry.

Antal, James A. *Considering a New Call: Ethical and Spiritual Challenges for Clergy.* Bethesda, Md.: The Alban Institute, 2000.

> Written especially for the pastor who is "feeling the itch" to move to a different congregation, this book explores the sensitive issues of confidentiality and ethics as one discerns the directions of one's call and explores possibilities with other congregations. An

appendix addresses how these issues directly affect search committees.

Avery, William O. *Revitalizing Congregations: Refocusing and Healing through Pastoral Transitions.* Bethesda, Md.: The Alban Institute, 2002.

As noted above, trained interim pastors can make all the difference in preparing the path for a ministry transition. This book tells stories of six congregations that successfully navigated this in-between time with the help of a skilled interim pastor.

Macy, Ralph. *The Interim Pastor.* Bethesda, Md.: The Alban Institute, 1986.

A good brief introduction to interim ministry and understanding its function and value to a congregation seeking a new pastor. Available online only at www.alban.org.

Mead, Loren B. *A Change of Pastors...and How It Affects Change in the Congregation.* Herdon, Va., 2005.

In this updated and revised edition of his book, *Critical Moment of Ministry,* Mead helps clergy understand the process parish members go through before a new pastor arrives and gives lay members guidance on taking advantage of this fertile time for change in the congregation.

Nicholson, Roger S., ed. *Temporary Shepherds: A Congregational Handbook for Interim Ministry.* Bethesda, Md.: The Alban Institute, 1998.

This is the standard text on interim ministry, written by a dozen experienced interim pastors. Both lay leaders and interim ministers will find this book to be indispensable.

Oswald, Roy M. *Crossing the Boundary between Seminary and Parish.* Bethesda, Md.: The Alban Institute, 1993.

Based on an early Alban Institute research project, this document still provides essential information on understanding the challenges of moving out of the seminary environment and into congregational leadership. Available online only at www.alban.org.

———. *New Beginnings: The Pastorate Start-up Workbook.* Washington, D.C.: Alban Institute, 1989.

Oswald provides helpful resources to assist pastors understand their leadership and entry styles, to build support systems, and to do the essential self-care to overcome the stress and strain of making a transition.

———. *Running through the Thistles: Terminating a Ministerial Relationship with a Parish.* Washington, D.C.: The Alban Institute, 1978.

A clear, brief exploration of termination styles and how they can effect both the pastor and the congregation.

Oswald, Roy M., and Robert E. Friedrich, Jr. *Discerning Your Congregation's Future: A Strategic and Spiritual Approach.* Bethesda, Md.: The Alban Institute, 1996.

Although not written specifically for congregations undergoing a pastoral transition, this book provides useful guides to discerning where your church is being called to go, which can in turn help shape the pastoral search profile.

Oswald, Roy M., James M. Heath, and Ann W. Heath. *Beginning Ministry Together: The Alban Handbook for Clergy Transitions.* Herndon, Va.: The Alban Institute, 2003.

This new resource is another essential text for churches undergoing a pastoral change, as it explores every step of the process and the key tasks that pastors, lay leaders, search committees, and judicatories must tackle to ensure successful transitions.

Rendle, Gilbert R. *Leading Change in the Congregation: Spiritual and Organizational Tools for Leaders.* Bethesda, Md.: The Alban Institute, 1998.

Another book not written directly at churches undergoing pastoral changes, but a wonderful guide to understanding the dynamics of change and how it can be navigated successfully.

Rendle, Gilbert R., and Alice Mann. *Holy Conversations: Strategic Planning as a Spiritual Practice for Congregations.* Bethesda, Md.: The Alban Institute, 2003.

This book is a compendium of some of the best knowledge available on designing a process not just for strategic planning but for understanding God's direction for your congregation and acting upon it.

Vonhof, John. *The Alban Guide to Managing the Pastoral Search Process.* Bethesda, Md.: The Alban Institute, 1999.

An eminently practical guidebook to managing every step of the pastoral search, with great ideas on handling paperwork, working with a search team, and communicating with the congregation.

White, Edward A., ed. *Saying Goodbye: A Time of Growth for Congregations and Pastors.* Bethesda, Md.: The Alban Institute, 1990.

Some of the best advice available on making a "good goodbye," which shows some keen understanding on the emotions that accompany this change. This book also includes examples of a farewell worship service and a litany for the closing of a ministry.

About the Authors

As an independent consultant and trainer in Organization Development, Bunty Ketcham serves organizations and individuals who are considering or are in the midst of major transitions. Formerly a member of the trainer network of the Mid-Atlantic Association for Training and Consulting (MATC) and of the Consultant Services Corps of the Central Atlantic Conference of the United Church of Christ, she presently serves in the Consultant Services Network of the Episcopal Diocese of Washington. She can be reached at: Bunty Ketcham & Associates, 2 East Melrose Street, Chevy Chase, Maryland 20815; (301) 652-0325; oketcham@hotmail.com.

Celia Allison Hahn is former editor-in-chief at the Alban Institute and is the author of *Understanding Your Church's Hidden Spirit* (Alban, 2001), among other publications. She lives in Washington, D.C.